M000032214

# CRAPPER CYCLE LANES

## 50 MORE OF THE WORST BIKE LANES IN BRITAIN

BIZARRE BIKING

Published by Eye Books Ltd.

29 Barrow Street
Much Wenlock
Shropshire
TF13 6EN

**www.eye-books.com**

First published in Great Britain 2016

**© Eye Books**

Written and designed by David Whelan for Eye Books

This book was inspired by the Facility of the Month feature on the
Warrington Cycle Campaign website.

The events and opinions in this book originate from the author. The
publisher accepts no responsibility for their accuracy.

The moral right of David Whelan to be identified as the author of this
work has been asserted by him in accordance with the Copyright,
Design and Patents Act, 1988.

# eye**Opener**

It was nearly 10 years ago that Eye Books published the first Crap Cycle Lanes book based on the "Facility of the Month" website pages of Warrington Cycle Campaign. Since 2001 this has featured pictures of badly designed cycle provision every month. Normally when introducing a sequel to a publication a foreword would say how delighted the authors are to be able to continue their previous publishing success. But in the case of Crap Cycle Lanes and its sequel, Crapper Cycle Lanes, this foreword has to be tinged with some regret that such monstrosities are still being foisted on the UK population.

So, this book is testament to the continuing ability of traffic authorities to get things wrong by putting in cycle facilities that fail the functionality, practicality and sometimes safety test.

We should note, however, that improvements have been made in places, and some cycle facilities are excellent. We like to feel the warm glow of satisfaction that maybe our little book helped in some way.

In our 2007 publication we called for the implementation

of 20mph speed limits as the default for urban roads. In November 2007 20's Plenty for Us was set up to assist community campaigners who wanted 20mph limits and now over 320 local campaign groups have been formed around the UK as of September 2016. In fact this has been widely adopted by local authorities with most of the UK's iconic cities now setting 20mph limits for most roads. Now 16m people live in such places and our call is for this to become the national default. Wide-area 20mph limits have become best practice for making our streets better places to walk and cycle. See much more at www.20splenty.org

So please enjoy this book, we hope it will be the last of its kind we ever need to publish.

**Rod King MBE**
*Warrington Cycle Campaign,*
*Founder - 20's Plenty for Us*

**With special thanks** to: Pete Owens

And to our other contributors:
Adam Edwards, Adrian Botting, Aisling Spain, Alan Gibson, Andrew Cosgrove, Andy Flanagan, Bernard Frippiat, Bill Gannon, Bogus Zaba, Bruce Poole, Damian Miles, Dave Brown, Dermott Ryan, Gary Outram, Geoff Holt, Geraint Jones, Helen Simmons, Jane Durney, John Meudell, Jonathan Robson, Kathryn Montgomery, Mark O'Donnell, Mark Strong, Matt Gill, Matthew Clark, Matthew Phillips, Matthew Stephenson, Niall Leonard, Peter Dupont , Peter Smith, Rebecca Lawson, Rob Kingston, Rob O'Brien, Rob Wood, Robert Evans, Roger Hill, Ros Gasson, S Archer, Stephen Shrubsall, Stevie Down, Terry Patterson, Tim Burford and Freddy,

thank you for all of the excellent contributions.

# QUALITY

Look at these. Aren't they beautiful? Right outside Old Trafford football stadium, home of world-famous Manchester United, they bestride and fairly grace a stretch of National Cycle Route 55.

These gleaming examples of street impedimentia are so finely fashioned, so meticulously maintained, and of such obviously superior material that it would be a privilege to have your knees and nadgers mashed upon them.

And, look at the brash bright green cycle path. The assurance with which it disdains the kerb and its feeble attempt to sway the unerring course of this heroic lane as it bravely and angularly bestrides four lanes of traffic.

This, surely, is heroic street furniture.

**HAZARD LEVEL**: LUNCH LOSS

# GOOF LEVEL:
## GOVEY

**CRAPPER CYCLE LANES**

**PROPOSED REMEDY**
## SPECIAL MEASURES

# SUPERHIGHWAY SUSPENDED

Here's another site benefiting from "improvement". On Southwark Bridge, crossing the mighty Thames into the City of London, cyclists have a very decent braking distance to stop and are brightly advised of the impending suspension of normal service.

There is, as we see, just enough room to swerve around the finely-sharpened edges of the sign, leaving a phalanx of commuter cyclists no choice but to pile straight into you.

How wonderfully almost all of London is 'improving.' i.e., fenced off and not working.

**HAZARD LEVEL:** BUTTOCK TENSION

# GOOF LEVEL: NIGEL

CYCLISTS
ADVANCE WARNING
CYCLE LANE
CLOSED AHEAD

CRAPPER CYCLE LANES

PROPOSED REMEDY
ADMINISTRATION

# MORE BIKING
# IN YOUR BIKING

You love to cycle, I love to cycle. We all love to cycle. So, what can be better than 50 metres of cycle path? Half a kilometre of cycle path, obviously. Stockton Council found the opportunity near Ingleby Barwick to add considerably to the cycling pleasures of the locality and consume a couple of otherwise useless little tracts of land in the process.

Our intrepid photographer, Stevie Down, took a simpler alternative and bounced straight over the top, snapping this handy pic mid-hop. Don't try this at home, kids.

**HAZARD LEVEL: BREATH CATCH**

# GOOF LEVEL: JEREMY

CRAPPER CYCLE LANES

## PROPOSED REMEDY
# NEGATIVE INTEREST

# DANCE IN A TRANCE

Bournemouth has many wonderful sights to see, and visiting cyclists can partake of the local magic with this handy diversion around a picturesque old pole.

It's a refreshing relief from a cycle lane that would otherwise lead so monotonously from one side of this junction all the way to the other.

The cyclist can now enjoy the sights and take the sea air before rejoining the throng on this scenic route.

**HAZARD LEVEL:** BREATH CATCH

# GOOF LEVEL: NIGEL

CRAPPER CYCLE LANES

**PROPOSED REMEDY**
# SPECIAL MEASURES

# DEPARTING ON THE LEFT, IS NOW DEPARTING ON THE RIGHT

Along with other innovative traffic measures, planners in Holland have made considerable successes by removing obstacles on the road and pavement and reducing demarcation between different classes of street user. Pedestrians, motor vehicles and bicycles are left with more autonomy to negotiate their own space.

This has brought improved road safety, and that's normally attributed to people taking more care. Camden Council strenuously applied this logic to Tavistock Place and reasoned that what made people take more care was a constant state of low-level bafflement.

**HAZARD LEVEL: HEART TREMOR**

# GOOF LEVEL:

## BORIS

Not known to do things by half, Camden opted for quite a high-level bafflement, applying lane-flipping multi-directional contraflow reversal without warning and for no discernible reason.

## PROPOSED REMEDY
### ADMINISTRATION

# SHORT STAY

Leicester City Council realises that cyclists need respite, rest. Some space to recuperate. A cycle lane that's so relaxing there isn't room to ride the whole length of your bike. Thoughtfully, they provide the lane in both directions.

Try not to break the speed limit.

**HAZARD LEVEL:** LUNCH LOSS

# GOOF LEVEL: GOVEY

CRAPPER CYCLE LANES

PROPOSED REMEDY
INSPECTORS VISIT

# STEPPING UP

Riding bicycles up and down steps is not good for the rims of the wheels. It's not particularly good for the rider, either. That may in part account for why this presumably well-intentioned cycle parking facility at Sheffield University is so cruelly spurned. Still, it means there is usually a space free if you need one.

**HAZARD LEVEL:** LUNCH LOSS

# GOOF LEVEL:
## NIGEL

**PROPOSED REMEDY**
## SPECIAL MEASURES

CRAPPER CYCLE LANES

# PRECIOUS MOMENTS

"Is this the beginning," sang achingly romantic 1980s disco trio The Three Degrees, "Or is this the end?"

There's no disputing that this facility near Andover in Hampshire is very clearly marked. That's stated here under the rule that if you have nothing nice to say, you should say nothing. And there really is very little else that we can say.

Does this represent the precise length of cycle lane allocation that the local authority had left over to provide at the end of one frayed financial year? Was this facility in the process of being laid out in 2007, on the day before a fat banker ran away with all the city's money? The cycling public, as the saying goes, have a right to know.

**HAZARD LEVEL:** BREATH CATCH

# GOOF LEVEL: BORIS

END

CRAPPER CYCLE LANES

PROPOSED REMEDY
INSPECTORS VISIT

# REFUGE

Busy traffic on Blackfriars Bridge Road can be hazardous for rush-hour cyclists. Ever-caring Southwark Council have made two hundred yards of cycle path provision along the central reservation just to offer that little extra security.

All the commuting London cyclist needs to do is to cross three lanes of busy traffic to get there, then cycle in serene splendour those two hundred magnificent yards before braving the dash across the next three lanes of screaming traffic.

**HAZARD LEVEL:** BUTTOCK TENSION

# GOOF LEVEL:
## JEREMY

**PROPOSED REMEDY**
## NEGATIVE INTEREST

# HEIDEGGER, HEIDEGGER WAS A BOOZY BEGGAR

The cyclist's lot in London is one of intense, forced concentration on the immediate. The physical. Too rarely is she, or he, intellectually taxed and presented with a real existential challenge. In Clapham, Lambeth offer a puzzle to match Descartes's question or Hamlet's dilemma.

A cycle path on which cycling is forbidden.

Immanuel Kant was a real piss-ant.

HAZARD LEVEL: LUNCH LOSS

# GOOF LEVEL:
## GOVEY

CRAPPER CYCLE LANES

**PROPOSED REMEDY**
## INSPECTORS VISIT

# MEMORIES
# ARE MADE OF THIS

Students at the Whitgift School in Croydon will have precious, innocent memories to share with their children and grandchildren. The tales they will have to tell of lazy summer days and brisk winter mornings when they cycled carefree, en masse, up and down the whole of this fabulous, five-metre facility.

Ah, the flower of youth, cycling, cloistered in a cage of protective bollards, all the way from quite near the school to not very much further away from the school, secure and unperturbed by cars, buses, trucks, pedestrians, prams, horses, yeti or pachyderms.

**HAZARD LEVEL:** BREATH CATCH

# GOOF LEVEL: NIGEL

CRAPPER CYCLE LANES

**PROPOSED REMEDY**
# ADMINISTRATION

# STUNT TRAINING

Mold Valley planning department recently realised how flimsy and insubstantial these cycle parking racks were and upgraded them to the far more robust street furniture we see now.

Fortunately, they didn't diminish the thrill-ride element of this facility. Coming off a nice incline, the cycle racks are followed within centimetres by a metre and a half plunge. If that isn't exciting enough, right nearby is a steep and narrow flight of steps for you to plunge down headlong.

**HAZARD LEVEL: AIR AMBULANCE**

# GOOF LEVEL:

## DONALD
### PANIC

## PROPOSED REMEDY
### JEREMY HUNT

# UNCIVIL UNENGINEERING

It looks as though an angry god arrived in the middle of the Cold War, threw around some concrete and masonry, then left in a huff. Leicestershire authorities have taken the architectural term "brutalism" and added aggressive and antisocial damage to what is normally known as "civil" engineering.

**HAZARD LEVEL:** HEART TREMOR

# GOOF LEVEL:
## JEREMY

CRAPPER CYCLE LANES

PROPOSED REMEDY
INSPECTORS VISIT

# INFINITY AND BEYOND

Not so much a cycle lane, more an on-ramp to the hereafter. Launching at a brave and jaunty angle into Guilford's bus traffic and right in the path of hastily parked Peggy Door-Flinga, this suddenly abbreviated cycling route offers a pathway to paradise. A sudden and complete opportunity to forget your debts, regrets and woes, once and for all.

Nice going, Guildford. This one's very literally a double whammy with an angular artistic twist.

**HAZARD LEVEL:** AIR AMBULANCE

# GOOF LEVEL:

## BORIS

**PROPOSED REMEDY**
## ADMINISTRATION

CRAPPER CYCLE LANES

CRAPPER CYCLE LANES

# CHOICE

No town planner can know when things will all become too much for a weary cyclist, but in Solihull, as in a few boroughs we'll see throughout this volume, the good aldermen and officers realise that a biker may just want to give it all up and rest his or her legs. To relax and take the bus.

Bikes aren't allowed on buses, of course, so you'll have to abandon your Cannondale or your Trek by the side of the road, but at least there's a bus stop nearby so you have that choice.

**HAZARD LEVEL:** LUNCH LOSS

# GOOF LEVEL: GOVEY

CRAPPER CYCLE LANES

PROPOSED REMEDY
INSPECTORS VISIT

# PACING

While it's a fun, healthy and relaxing form of transport, never forget that cycling is serious exercise. It's a workout for your whole body. With this in mind, Galway have provided regular enforced breaks to ensure that cyclists stop for a breather, at least as often as is necessary.

They've also provided innumerable opportunities for cyclists and emerging car drivers to encounter one another. Suddenly.

**HAZARD LEVEL: BUTTOCK TENSION**

# GOOF LEVEL: NIGEL

**PROPOSED REMEDY**
## SPECIAL MEASURES

CRAPPER CYCLE LANES

# ALTERNATIVE ROUTE

A break in the battle, a pause in the fight. Heavy goods and commercial traffic in Seaford can be wearing and jar the nerves. The planning department, ever eager to lessen the load of the weary traveller, furnished these eight or nine yards as a space in which you can cast off the cares and ride away, out of the fray.

From the combination of the markings and the sign, it's not quite obvious whether the cycle lane is a facility shared with the pedestrians and their young ones who do, quite honestly, look to be in some peril from airborne pedallers.

**HAZARD LEVEL:** LUNCH LOSS

# GOOF LEVEL: NIGEL

**PROPOSED REMEDY**
## NEGATIVE INTEREST

CRAPPER CYCLE LANES

# MEDALLING

Ah. The Olympics, 2012. The opening ceremony. The Olympic Park. Anish Kapoor's helter-skelter. (He doesn't like you to call it that, you know. Even now, when it actually is a helter-skelter.) The velodrome. And, right outside, this brave, brilliant, yet, baffling bit of bureaucratic brainstorm.

Still, there is no parking allowed. So you should always be sure of a clear run all the way from nowhere very much to nowhere else at all. Just long enough to wonder why it was that so many people were keen to say "medalling" for the London games. And how they all seemed to come to their senses and stop at the same time.

**HAZARD LEVEL:** BREATH CATCH

# GOOF LEVEL: BORIS

**PROPOSED REMEDY: ADMINISTRATION**

CRAPPER CYCLE LANES

# COMMITMENT

This cycle lane, less than a metre wide, is the supreme test of testosterone. Yes, lady cyclists have testosterone, too. But you knew that. And you'll need it. When two cycles approach each other here in Holyrood Park, especially after a bevy or two, one of them is going to wind up like the black knight in *Monty Python and the Holy Grail*. Limbless, bouncing and shouting, "None shall pass! It's only a flesh wound! Come back here and I'll bite yer kneecaps!"

Bicycle jousting doesn't get the recognition that it deserves. Edinburgh's efforts should surely help it to qualify as an Olympic sport.

**HAZARD LEVEL**: BUTTOCK TENSION

# GOOF LEVEL:
## NIGEL

CYCLE WAY

CYCLE
WAY

CRAPPER CYCLE LANES

**PROPOSED REMEDY**
**INSPECTORS VISIT**

# SPARE US THE GUTTER

Liverpool? Check. Liverpudlian musical reference stroke song title in the headline? Check. But it's not the Beatles. Oh, no. See, we're better than that. And we're not going to say, "All right, all right, calm down," nor, "Who's nicked half me bike lane, then? Eh? Eh?" neither. Oh, okay. Maybe we are.

Here's the thing – Liverpool City councillors please take note: If you don't have room for the little symbolic drawing of a bicycle, which you will have noticed is rather smaller than an actual bicycle, then there won't be space for, say, a bicycle, will there? I mean it stands to reason, doesn't it.

**HAZARD LEVEL:** HEART TREMOR

# GOOF LEVEL:

## NIGEL

CRAPPER CYCLE LANES

# KINETIC DIVERSION

Along this excellent and regularly maintained new facility in Canning Town, cyclists and motor traffic alike are given good early warning of an impending diversion. Motor vehicles will be diverted at the next junction to an alternative road route.

Cyclists are automatically diverted skywards.

**HAZARD LEVEL: BUTTOCK TENSION**

# GOOF LEVEL:
## NIGEL

Diverted
traffic

**PROPOSED REMEDY**
## ADMINISTRATION

CRAPPER CYCLE LANES

# RUMBLE BUM

Modern cycle paths all too often lack kinetic, tactile feedback for riders. Advanced engineering from the boffins among the dreaming spires of the university town of Oxford provides this helpful lunch-loosening cycle lane with a thrilling downhill incline.

As the photograph demonstrates, the lane is well-used by pedestrians. Cyclists appear less entralled in this morning shot.

Maybe the thrilling vibrobum effect is more popular on the homeward journey, after work.

**HAZARD LEVEL:** LUNCH LOSS

# GOOF LEVEL: GOVEY

**CRAPPER CYCLE LANES**

**PROPOSED REMEDY**
**SPECIAL MEASURES**

# SHARED FACILITY

An opportunity to show off your truly spectacular bunny hops to a clutch of morning commuters as they yawn and await the bus. Or, if you don't feel up to mounting and clearing the bus stop, there's a chance to swerve and potentially slice through said commuters.

See how a little imaginative planning can turn the dullest road into a potential disaster movie.

**HAZARD LEVEL:** BREATH CATCH

# GOOF LEVEL:
## NIGEL

**PROPOSED REMEDY**
## INSPECTORS VISIT

# LOW FLYING BIKES

Torbay Council in Devon caters for the very particular wants and needs of holidaymakers in Paignton. Apparently a popular leisure pursuit is to view the undersides of bicycles as they leap over amassed and serried loungers. This is a warm-up, in preparation for the jump they'll shortly make over the fishing huts.

Paignton is one of the few fine English seaside resorts where cyclists are known to snatch fish and chips back from the seagulls overhead.

It's a kind of supersized vibration strip. Or a Hornby Double-O gauge miniature riding experience akin to the streets of San Francisco.

## HAZARD LEVEL: BUTTOCK TENSION

# GOOF LEVEL:
# JEREMY

CRAPPER CYCLE LANES

**PROPOSED REMEDY**
# NEGATIVE INTEREST

# ACADEMIC PUZZLE

In the county that boasts Stephen Hawking as Lucasian Professor of Mathematics, you'd expect something a little above and beyond the ordinary in a cycle facility. Here in leafy Ely, cycling is at once both provisioned and prohibited. Cyclists are required to adhere strictly to Heisenberg's uncertainty principle: to be, like quarks or Schrödinger's cat, unknowable.

Present, perhaps, but only when they are unobserved.

**HAZARD LEVEL:** BREATH CATCH

# GOOF LEVEL:
## GOVEY

**PROPOSED REMEDY**
## SPECIAL MEASURES

# THIS CYCLE LANE IS NO MORE

An excellent cycle path network runs from north Liverpool into the city centre. Where it ceases to be excellent. In fact it abruptly ceases to be. And that may be what cyclists, or at least their bicycles, are expected to do. Mounting the pavement, is, of course, unthinkable. And illegal. As it would be to continue into the path of the oncoming traffic. Illegal and quite lethal.

And so there is, presumably, at this point, a Stargate through which cyclists pass, although the Highway Code prescribed symbol for a Stargate doesn't feature in most editions. Perhaps that's why we don't see it on the signpost here. There are other occasions where the sign would come in handy. As we shall be able to see, a little later on.

**HAZARD LEVEL:** BUTTOCK TENSION

# GOOF LEVEL:
## NIGEL

CRAPPER CYCLE LANES

PROPOSED REMEDY
INSPECTORS VISIT

# KEEP THEM GUESSING

Pity the poor, overheated, bored travellers trapped in their motor vehicles. It must be so tedious for them as the endless stream of cyclists speeds by in the far left lane, leaving them trapped to swelter in their little sweat boxes. Town planners in Cambridge, like other imaginative council officers around the country, relieve that tedium by moving the cycle paths to random slots along the road. This provides an alternative to the games of "yellow car", "I spy" and "RTA rubber neck" that can all get so samey so soon.

This particular variation also provides cyclists with a thrilling game of "which Wally?" as they try to guess which Wally will fling open their car door without looking.

# HAZARD LEVEL: AIR AMBULANCE

# GOOF LEVEL:
## JEREMY

CRAPPER CYCLE LANES

**PROPOSED REMEDY**
## ADMINISTRATION

# ALL-TERRAIN COMMUTE

Here's a nice surprise provided by the Datchet local planning authority. Along the dull, featureless and mundane cycle path is an off-road opportunity about a metre and a half long. Commute, commute, commute, and then, just for a moment, mountain biking! Commute, commute, commute.

**HAZARD LEVEL:** LUNCH LOSS

# GOOF LEVEL: NIGEL

**PROPOSED REMEDY**
## INSPECTORS VISIT

CRAPPER CYCLE LANES

# TRAINING PLACES

Loughborough Council provides a superb training program to help cyclists improve their skills. Here, the cycle lane, already narrow by most standards, tapers to a challenging width.

Shortly afterwards, expect a swift downhill "Hands Free" zone, followed by a 10-cm wide "wheelies and Uni's only" slalom.

**HAZARD LEVEL:** BUTTOCK TENSION

# GOOF LEVEL: NIGEL

**PROPOSED REMEDY**
## INSPECTORS VISIT

CRAPPER CYCLE LANES

# SORRY QUAYS

Now That's What I Call a Crap Cycle Lane.

It's wide. We want to take this opportunity to observe how luxuriously wide the cycle facility is. Look. Mmmm. *Wiiiiide*. What other good thing can we say? It's quite leafy.

No doubt, Transport For London will have this spectacular cycling opportunity incorporated as a showpiece feature of the East-West Cycle Superhighway [CS3].

**HAZARD LEVEL:** LUNCH LOSS

# GOOF LEVEL:
## BORIS

CRAPPER CYCLE LANES

**PROPOSED REMEDY**
## NEGATIVE INTEREST

# STUMPED

Perhaps an end of fiscal year bollard surplus bonanza led to this intriguing torture feature, brought to you by the good burghers of Camden Town. There should be a prize for anyone who can cycle through this cunningly planned maze of metal with their knees and all their bits intact.

# GOOF LEVEL:

## GOVEY

PROPOSED REMEDY

COUNCELLING

# IF YOU HIT IT FAST ENOUGH AND AT JUST THE RIGHT ANGLE...

This looks like one of those places where the government is doing something secret. Along the National Cycle Network Route near Swansea, you have the opportunity to see just what it is they're getting up to. All you have to do is cycle through this concrete wall. It appears that a tunnel was excavated here, but owing to an administrative error – the entrance was fashioned in solid concrete.

**HAZARD LEVEL:** LUNCH LOSS

# GOOF LEVEL:

## NIGEL

CRAPPER CYCLE LANES

**PROPOSED REMEDY**
# INSPECTORS VISIT

# BEAUTY IN SYMMETRY

Rhythm and rigor in aesthetics are often marginalised as priorities for town planners. So very frequently, their endeavours are decried as mundane, faceless. Dull, even.

Not here in Warrington. Lo, aloft, the sign is held, beckoning bikers forth. How perfectly these bollards bestride the sweep of Warrington's Cuerdley Road. So admirably rhythmic is the pace that is set in their precise positioning, with a mathematical beauty that surely far surpasses the minor discomfort of a cracked patella or an impacted testicle.

**HAZARD LEVEL:** BUTTOCK TENSION

# GOOF LEVEL:

## NIGEL

CRAPPER CYCLE LANES

**PROPOSED REMEDY**
## SPECIAL MEASURES

# WET, WINDY AND WINDING

A scenic sweep to rival the Corniche in the South of France, or even the Cornish Riviera in the South of England, old Colwyn Promenade in the north of Wales gives a marvellous view of the beautiful bay at any time of day. But how thoughtful of the town planners to provide this teasing, testing, twisty trail to keep riders' concentration in sharp focus.

Exactly how the precise geometry of this thrilling route was devised is a secret that remains sealed in the council's vaults. Maybe some Druidic ritual, a Wiccan incantation, or an arcane Euclidean formula guided these unique, surprising swerves. Or maybe they just like a drink in North Wales. Who knows? But don't take one yourself if you're going to ride this route, especially at night. Only a few feet away, that lovely bay is on the edge of the Irish Sea. That's cold, that is.

**HAZARD LEVEL:** HEART TREMOR

# GOOF LEVEL:
## BORIS

CRAPPER CYCLE LANES

PROPOSED REMEDY
## ADMINISTRATION

# NOTHING TO IT

The trick with this little tease, on the otherwise serene and placid Trans Pennine Trail, is to send the bike through upside down, so the handlebars will fit in that gap while you simply vault the obstacle. Points will be awarded for style as well as for survival.

The object of the inverted stile, obviously, is to save cyclists from being jostled by moto-cross and other off-road motorcycles. Cunning planning ensures that jostling is almost out of the question.

High-speed, swerving side-swipe collisions are quite likely, though, as the tracks clearly show.

**HAZARD LEVEL:** LUNCH LOSS

# GOOF LEVEL:
# JEREMY

**PROPOSED REMEDY**
**INSPECTORS VISIT**

CRAPPER CYCLE LANES

# MINIATURE MULTI-TASKING MIRACLE

We have art, abstract design, an existential puzzle and at the same time, an outstandingly pointless consumption of clearly surplus Derbyshire County Council budget. The officers are to be congratulated, of course, for their considerations of safety and convenience in ensuring 24-hour prohibition of both parking and loading all the way around this outstanding facility.

**HAZARD LEVEL:** BREATH CATCH

# GOOF LEVEL:
## GOVEY

CRAPPER CYCLE LANES

**PROPOSED REMEDY**
## INSPECTORS VISIT

# POSITIVE FEEDBACK

Don't miss the thoughtful inclusion of the kinetic feedback paving, there to helpfully warn you with a rumble and a rut, were you to cycle on the wrong side of this shared bicycle and pedestrian route. While you're whacking your wobbly bits into the also kinetic cross-bar, it's good to know that a ready supply of dog poo is regularly replenished on the facility.

Chesterfield Town Council would be the place to address your letters of appreciation.

**HAZARD LEVEL:** BUTTOCK TENSION

# GOOF LEVEL:

## NIGEL

**CRAPPER CYCLE LANES**

**PROPOSED REMEDY**
## HEALTH INSPECTORS VISIT

# SALAD DAZE

Few town and road-planning authorities have the compassion and foresight to provide turn-offs, lay-bys for bikers. Resting places for sandwich breaks along the course of a cycle lane. Off the Maultway near Deepcut, this little lay-by is just big enough for a cyclist, a bike and a picnic.

Perfect, after the two or three yards of exhausting pedalling it will have taken to get there. Like so many of the far-sighted and adventurous facilities saluted by our humble little book, entrance to this cycle lane is from space.

Remember to bring a hot air balloon for your departure.

**HAZARD LEVEL:** BREATH CATCH

# GOOF LEVEL:
## GOVEY

**PROPOSED REMEDY**
## SPECIAL MEASURES

CRAPPER CYCLE LANES

# HUM A FEW BARS

As this picture clearly shows, the task of keeping the markings of a well-used cycle path constantly refreshed is well-nigh impossible. An imaginative alternative, developed by Kent County Council, is this audible and kinetic reminder that makes a delightful 'F-R-R-R-R' sound as your elbows and knees scrape along its boingy length.

Musicians will immediately appreciate that varying the speed of your passage will raise and lower the pitch of vibration, which will enable any decently skilled cyclist to produce something of a tune with which to entertain the passing traffic.

**HAZARD LEVEL**: AIR AMBULANCE

# GOOF LEVEL:
## NIGEL

CRAPPER CYCLE LANES

**PROPOSED REMEDY**
## ADMINISTRATION

# GATHERING NUTS

Squirrels need cycle paths, too. Apparently.

Transport for London, having obviously completed all of the possible facilities that human cyclists in London could ever need, trialled this rodent facility in Boston Manor, should soon be set to announce forthcoming bike lanes for urban foxes, too, in a city-wide roll-out.

**HAZARD LEVEL:** BREATH CATCH

# GOOF LEVEL:

## GOVEY

**PROPOSED REMEDY**
### ADMINISTRATION

**CRAPPER CYCLE LANES**

# PATH WITH A VIEW

Obviously, this pavement is way too narrow for pedestrians to be safe with oncoming cyclists sharing the space. The sign, however, could be clearer, in indicating that the top of the narrow wall is the cycle-lane provision. Offering, as it does, unparallelled views over the Tyne, the vista can sweep from Byker to Gateshead on a clear day, and maybe even offer a glimpse of the Baltic Centre for Contemporary Art.

**HAZARD LEVEL:** AIR AMBULANCE

# GOOF LEVEL:

## DONALD PANIC

CRAPPER CYCLE LANES

**PROPOSED REMEDY**
## JEREMY HUNT

# BUFFERING

One thing that will muck up any cycle ride and ruin any peaceful journey, is a flaky Wi-Fi signal and the awful judder that grinds Netflix. Spotify won't drop out in the middle of your commute along this crinkly path in Fleet in Hampshire. Oh, no.

The story goes that a US aircraft carrier encountered another vessel in fog. By radio, the carrier announced, "This is the *USS Nimitz* approaching. Steer left 15°".

The response came, "Collision possible. Recommend you steer left 15°".

The captain of the carrier took the radio, "I repeat, this is the *USS Nimitz* approaching. We are an aircraft carrier, the second largest vessel in the United States naval fleet. Steer left 15° or collision is possible."

And the reply: "This is a lighthouse. Your call".

**HAZARD LEVEL:** LUNCH LOSS

# GOOF LEVEL:
## NIGEL

PROPOSED REMEDY
INSPECTORS VISIT

CRAPPER CYCLE LANES

# SOMETHING TO WRAP YOUR HEAD AROUND

Or maybe a chance to show your pole-dancing moves. The planners of Farnborough have imposed a very definite stop here.

Perhaps it's to calm the raging cycle traffic and enforce a pause while you await the passage of workers at the Hawley trading estate or parties of visiting schoolchildren or the herds of migratory wildebeest for which Farnborough is so widely famed.

Or it could be that the pole is there solely to direct your attention skywards so as not to miss the annual air show.

**HAZARD LEVEL:** BUTTOCK TENSION

# GOOF LEVEL:

## NIGEL

CRAPPER CYCLE LANES

PROPOSED REMEDY
**NEGATIVE INTEREST**

# AND THERE'S EVEN
# A LANE FOR UNICYCLES

Cyclists come from all directions to the splendid Tesco in Illminster. (Splendid… Tesco. Now how is that supposed to work?) Well, apparently they check out anytime they want, but they can never leave. The signage doesn't give clear guidance over whether pedestrians are allowed to walk in both directions but cyclists, while they are encouraged to converge here, have no route for departure.

And why ever would they want one?

**HAZARD LEVEL:** LUNCH LOSS

# GOOF LEVEL:
## BORIS

PROPOSED REMEDY
THERAPY

# HOOP TOP

Say what you like about the hoop-topped bollard – and it gets a bad rap generally – but how far do you have to look these days to find somewhere to tie up your horse?

Oxford pedestrians love these little diversions. Apparently. So it seems they're easily amused. Quite what benefit anyone imagines there is in providing them in the middle of a cycle path remains something of a mystery, but life so often is that way, isn't it?

**HAZARD LEVEL:** LUNCH LOSS

# GOOF LEVEL: GOVEY

**PROPOSED REMEDY**
## SPECIAL MEASURES

CRAPPER CYCLE LANES

# SHARED USE

In Nottinghamshire, it's clearly and correctly been made a priority to provide a cycle lane that will not present a hazard to people waiting at a bus stop.

Nobody should want to make their lives any worse than they already are. They're waiting for a bus. Have a heart.

Luckily, the buses are so infrequent that they are unlikely to present too much of a hazard to the cyclists who may occasionally have to ride through them. Of course, bus vs cycle doesn't always end well, but town planning is a tricky business.

You simply can't please everyone.

**HAZARD LEVEL:** AIR AMBULANCE

# GOOF LEVEL:

# DONALD

**PROPOSED REMEDY**
# ADMINISTRATION

# TEST TRACK

Thinking of buying a new bike? Need somewhere to try it out, get the feel of it? Bring it to Croydon and cycle freely along these several smart metres of brightly painted, superbly-maintained showpiece cycling facilities.

You can ride unhindered from that nice parking control wallet-gouging box on the left, all the way to the next parking bay along.

HAZARD LEVEL: BREATH CATCH

# GOOF LEVEL:
## BORIS

**PROPOSED REMEDY**
## INSPECTORS VISIT

CRAPPER CYCLE LANES

# SURPRISE!

Swindon's not the kind of place you want to take at any speed. There's nowhere much to go, and really no reason to hurry getting there. And, if you were to get up any speed, you'd learn your lesson pretty soon. They don't hold with that sort of thing around here, and, quite honestly, why should they?

The bike lane does seem to come to a rather abrupt halt, but then it has entered a one-way street, going the other way. So. Bollards.

**HAZARD LEVEL:** AIR AMBULANCE

# GOOF LEVEL:

## JEREMY

CRAPPER CYCLE LANES

**PROPOSED REMEDY**
## RISK ASSESSMENT

# GOOD INTENTIONS

**CRAPPER CYCLE LANES**

This intricately planned and well-thought-out segregated cycle path facility, with crossing spaces for pedestrians, would be nearly perfect were it not for the teensy little detail that cyclists travelling one way in the direction this photograph was taken must prepare themselves for vertical bisection in order to complete the course.

Young BMX heroes, naturally, will be able to hop along the top of the otherwise inconvenient rail. Evolution in action.

HAZARD LEVEL: LUNCH LOSS

# GOOF LEVEL:
## GOVEY

**PROPOSED REMEDY**
## SPECIAL MEASURES

# BOLLARD AMONG BOLLARDS

When the London borough of Bromley raises a bollard, you know what they want it to be. A straight, no-nonsense bollard. A bollard that is no more and no less than that, a solid, unapologetic, belligerently obstructive assertion of a highway amenity.

And why should it not be exactly the same colour as the tarmac it inhabits? It's there to keep people, cyclists, children, anything with soft tissue, off the tarmac.

It's there to keep the tarmac from being sullied by your mucky tyres. Gertcha.

**HAZARD LEVEL:** BUTTOCK TENSION

# GOOF LEVEL:
## NIGEL

CRAPPER CYCLE LANES

## PROPOSED REMEDY
## REASSIGNMENT

# OMNI-CRUMPLES

A cutely narrow cycle lane, teasingly flaunted in the midst of the motor carriageway, grazing the edge of the parked car door flinging zone, that gives straight into the flow of the squeezed two-lane traffic chicane, disciplined with two built-out kerbs. Kingston-Upon-Thames is plainly overpopulated, and the local council are rightly determined to do something about it.

Opportunities for cyclists include the option to plough into the passengers of cars as they step carelessly out into the cycle path, or to mangle themselves on the edges of said doors. Bikers may bounce onto the bonnets and through the windscreens of oncoming cars, or simply cause the cars to crumple one another in their swerves to avoid pedestrians, cyclists, passengers and each other.

One way or another, there will be fewer people in this part of south London pretty soon.

**HAZARD LEVEL:** AIR AMBULANCE

# GOOF LEVEL:
## JEREMY

END
🚲

**PROPOSED REMEDY**
## PSYCHOLOGICAL EVALUATION

CRAPPER CYCLE LANES

# PASTORAL RETREAT

Away from the throng, the cut and thrust, the bustle of the Guilford pavement, this leafy idyll is a haven, a rural escape. Listen to the birds. Smell the wildflowers. Taste the early tang of spring on the breeze.

Here is a place where weary bikers can relax and recover for seven tranquil metres before returning, pitching back into the strife of the shared-use affray.

**HAZARD LEVEL:** BREATH CATCH

# GOOF LEVEL:

## GOVEY

**PROPOSED REMEDY**
# ADMINISTRATION

**CRAPPER CYCLE LANES**

# ON A DIME

Excellently designed for uni-cyclists, although you will need telepathic gifts or at the very least extraordinary foresight, to anticipate the stomach-wrenching right turn. The little beam-me-up pad on the pedestrian island is delightfully proportioned although steering around that pole requires some deft manoeuvres.

Aim the tractor beams at Loughborough Station, approached from the A60 Nottingham Road in Leicestershire, for your away-party to reach this unique location.

**HAZARD LEVEL: BUTTOCK TENSION**

# GOOF LEVEL: NIGEL

CRAPPER CYCLE LANES

PROPOSED REMEDY
INSPECTORS VISIT

# WHEN IS A CYCLE PATH NOT A CYCLE PATH?

This path is not only too narrow to cycle on comfortably, but uniquely in this collection, it's also too shallow.

Most cyclists would bang their shoulders and quite likely their heads in this creatively designated facility near the Greenfield Golf Course in Wolverhampton. It's probably just as well, because if people were walking through the tunnel in the opposite direction, somebody would get hurt.

By way of a small consolation, if you rode through the tunnel and made the passage unscathed, there's a lamppost you'd smack into right on the other side.

**HAZARD LEVEL:** LUNCH LOSS

# GOOF LEVEL: GOVEY

CRAPPER CYCLE LANES

**PROPOSED REMEDY**
**INSPECTORS VISIT**

# EVENHANDED

On a winding path where there are hedges, even in good light, the potential for head-on collision is always risky. For the pretty cycle path between Gibbons Close and Woodhouse Crescent, Telford & Wrekin Council have found an innovative solution.

Two cyclists approaching this curve from opposite directions will fairly certainly both smack into the telegraph pole, but on separate sides.

Thus any possible risk of them smacking into each other is averted.

**HAZARD LEVEL:** BUTTOCK TENSION

# GOOF LEVEL:

## BORIS

**PROPOSED REMEDY**
## SPECIAL MEASURES

CRAPPER CYCLE LANES

# HEALTH WARNING

There was in the past a lot of long, sorry, often unedifying debate about the hazards of passive smoking. On balance, prolonged passive exposure to other people's cigarette smoke may well have more lasting effects on one's health than active lamppost smacking.

Even if you crack your head open against the unwielding pole and die, it shouldn't take too long. Anyway, if you have the good sense to do it here under the very helpful sign, the A&E department is only about 30 metres away.

**HAZARD LEVEL:** LUNCH LOSS

# GOOF LEVEL: GOVEY

## PROPOSED REMEDY
### ADMINISTRATION

CRAPPER CYCLE LANES

# THE NEW WHACK

Black is so cool, isn't it? So relaxed. Such a statement. Stylish, yet unobtrusive. Almost invisible. Especially at night. The chance that Surrey County Council offer to cyclists in this creatively laid out facility is to discover whether black metal is softer against the forehead than a more brightly colored pole, and whether it tastes better.

If you find out, do let them know.

**HAZARD LEVEL:** HEART TREMOR

# GOOF LEVEL: NIGEL

## PROPOSED REMEDY
## INSPECTORS VISIT

CRAPPER CYCLE LANES

# ALL GOOD THINGS

In Enfield, road planners don't want you to be confused about whether the cycle lane has ended or not. They have a reserve plan: if this metal fence isn't sufficient to stop people cycling, they'll build a wall. And if that doesn't work, put spikes in the wall.

In Enfield, a cycle path can really only go so far. Apparently.

**HAZARD LEVEL:** LUNCH LOSS

# GOOF LEVEL: GOVEY

END

**PROPOSED REMEDY**
**INSPECTORS VISIT**

CRAPPER CYCLE LANES

CRAPPER CYCLE LANES

# IT'S A CYCLE LANE, JIM

But not as we know it. In the grounds of Finchley Memorial Hospital is what would've been a secret with the gravity of national security. The term "planners jape" has blown the cover, however, and now for all to see is the cycle entrance to the Frimley Stargate.

Whereabouts across the universe this particular Einstein Rosen bridge will land you is something no cyclist has yet to come back to say.

**HAZARD LEVEL:** BREATH CATCH

# GOOF LEVEL:
## BORIS

CRAPPER CYCLE LANES

## PROPOSED REMEDY
# ADMINISTRATION

# THIS IS THE END

A puzzling feature of this facility – a little outside the scope of this particular reference work – is: what kind of two-legged beasts are anticipated to regularly emerge from the murky depths here in Poole?

At least, whatever they are, they're a little more thoughtfully provided for than the cyclists who, as we've so often seen, are expected by the local council to arrange teleportation at quite short notice.

**HAZARD LEVEL:** POSSIBLE DROWNIN

# GOOF LEVEL: GOVEY

**CRAPPER CYCLE LANES**

**PROPOSED REMEDY**
## A SWIM

# eye**Bookshelf**

At Eye Books we publish books about ordinary people
doing extraordinary things.
Many of them involve bicycles.

## **Moods of Future Joys**
*Al Humphreys*
£9.99
ISBN: 978-1903070857

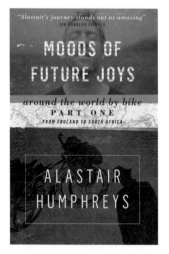

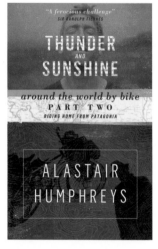

## **Thunder and Sunshine**
*Al Humphreys*
£9.99
ISBN: 978-1903070888

# BUY THESE GREAT BOOKS
*and more*

**Discovery Road**
*Andy Brown and Tim Garratt*
**£9.99**
ISBN: 978-1903070833

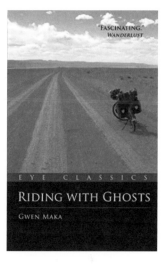

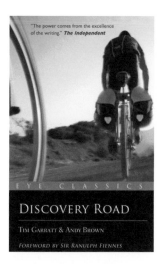

**Riding with Ghosts**
*Gwen Maka*
**£7.99**
ISBN: 978-1903070772

# www.eye-books.com